ALOHA MAHALO

(((Alejandro Saint-Barthélemy)))

ALOHA MAHALO

01001000
01100101
01101100
01101100
01101111

01110100
01101000
01100001
01101110
01101011
01110011

Aloha
(❀^‿^)
Mahalo.

MILLENNIAL CLICHÉ

i daydream with the day in which i could play FFVII without worrying about life, love, peace, war, the world, my city, time, Time…
well-to-do, retired, sit on a purple sofa, fluorescent green walls, a Darjeeling tea and vegan sushi on the table...

YOU ARE MY LONG LOST READER

You are my long lost reader and I
Will hug
Your shelfish
Heart
Very hard
Til we cry
2 glasses of
Champagne.

¯_(ツ)_/¯

BEST-SELLER

I don't want to dampen your enthusiasm but
I was butler-cum-gardener to Lady Jane
It's been infernally awkward even try to forget
I thought I'd never live it down.

Her nazi husband knew little
Casualties were miraculously light
The wreckage was borne away on the tide
Injured people were borne away in ambulances
The ferry was bearing down on us
After half an hour it was borne in on him
No one was listening.

A place inhabited by ghosts!
Man's inhumanity to man!
I was fortunate enough to escape!
The revolver bucked violently upwards!

To fire on all cylinders!!
To cut across a field!!
To have a tooth out!!
To be or not to be directionless!!
To have a foreboding that they still live...

[I still have to find a way to cut through
All this red tape \ (◎o◎) / !!!]

SIDDHARTHA

In the morning
In a dream
With my friend
Until the end.

The sun comes
The light shines
On a swimming pool
Hauntingly beautiful.

Beautiful love
Beautiful hate
In everything that exists
In the river every fish.

<(((">

5 MINUTES

Just 5 minutes to be alone with you
You'll find out I'm the one
Forget about her
Forget about him
Forget about the iPhone ringing.

Right now
I'm looking at a car parked on a street
There's a cat underneath
Which one would you like me to be?
The car, the cat or the street…

ヽ(´─`×)ノ

5W1H

Who is involved?
What to say?
When do we finish?
Where to look at?
Why so serious?
How come?

I just don't know what to do
With myself over you
While doing this thing
Called *fucking*.

¯_(ツ)_/¯

TAO LIN

tao lin is
my lost brother and i
will stab
my human heart
very hard
to make a smoothie
suitable for hamsters and dolphins
only.

¯_(ツ)_/¯

SELECTED TWEET

i will be unhappy until everybody else is happy but in the meantime i want my princess yacht too.

¯_(ツ)_/¯

AT 2:46 A.M.

My lover is mine, alright
Some of the time.

The future seems bright
The future seems fruitful
I think that's useful
Alright
All night
Tonight.

Move to another country
Start all over again
Not to get away
But to find something new
To find something else
And stay
Not pray
But play.

Maybe get a blowjob
Get stuff done.

Hug my wife
Forget the mistakes I've done.

Come on.

18

one day
18 years old
heading towards my grandma's
coming back from partying.

8 in the morning
sunday
winter
my mum's house had the keys in the door
didn't want to wake my family up
left on foot towards my grandma's
14km away
hangover
dejected
rejected
depressed
my first girlfriend had left me months ago
and i was not good at pickup.

i was a virgin
my girlfriend had left me because
i didn't fuck her
it took me a long time to understand this
and why that happens…

then

half-way through
freezing
hands in my pockets
blue jacket
i walked by a dog
a big one
and its female owner.

the dog didn't bark
then the woman told me:
he didnt bark at you!
he barks at everyone, you know?
he's really protective with me
but look!
he has put himself in front of you
protecting you!
would you like to come in?

no no no, thank you, i have to go
bye, take care
i said
like a retard.

nowadays i would have drilled her good.

back at the time
due to my shiness
and pristine sensitivity

i said *no*
yes
i said *no*.

then again
nowadays
that dog
would probably
bark at me

or not?…

¯_(ツ)_/¯

DES ESSEINTES

Hate
Retirement
Explosion in your eyes
You're 20 years old
And no more desire.

Lovers
Friends
Discotheques
You don't need no one of 'em.

A big house
In a quiet place
That's all you need
To rest.

Books
Films
Music
An escort sometimes
So unique.

Silence
Isolation
Freedom.

Mind to think
Soul to seek
Heart to reel.

Fruits
Grass
Flowers
Trees
Dew at dawn
The Nirvana is.

Glow-worms and moons
Seeds and skies
Singing with you at night
The Nirvana is…

☆ 彡 ☆ 三

MODERN HAIKU

health
wealth
love
happiness
red insects in an orgy on a white flower

BAD BLOOD BLUES

I feel like a feat
Every time I say to you
I love you
🎵🎵🎵

I am full of shit
I only love me
🎵🎵🎵

But it's you or nobody
So I'll keep lying
🎵🎵🎵

(´ー`)y-~~

BAD POETRY FOR BAD PEOPLE

I don't know why I can't cry
But I couldn't and I can't.

All the wanks watching lesbian porn
And all the feeling free
Sometimes they mean nothing to me
And it's only normal 'cause
They'll always be there for me.

When you smile
I don't mind smiling too
I don't mind lying for you
Well, not for you
Just for your four things:
Pretty ass
Sweet tongue
Shape body
Big tits.

Big tits in a shape body...

When you said last night
Goodnight and goodbye
It's all a mess
Time will tell the tale
Don't dream awake with me!

You were supposing I'm in love
And that's ok 'cause that's what
I've been pretending all along
But, you now know
I was saying to myself:
What a jerk!
I don't want her!
Just her blond hair!!
I don't want her to think nor feel!
Just a challenge getting her back to me!
A year later since I left her!
Fucking stupid frigid!!!

In this dirty old town
A man can't choose
A man can't choose
So if I can't get you back
I will lose
I will lose.

I'm a dead man!
Buried in porn and sad songs
If you say *No*
If you say *No*
If you say *No*
If you say *No*
If you say *No*.

I'm a dead man!
Buried in philosophy and ice creams
If you say *No* to me
If you say *No* to me
If you say *No* to me
If you say *No* to me
If you say *No* to me
If you say *No* to me
If you say *No* to me
If you say *No* to me
If you say *No* to me
If you say *No* to me.

\(o`Ⅲ'o)/

BARNEY STINSON

(Don't wanna know her
Don't wanna hold her
Just fuck
Just luck)

I wanna be with you all the time
Walking hand in hand through the park
Make you laugh out loud
Make you fall in love right now…

(Or just a half hour romp
Fucking hard in this park
Making her dam
Making her cum.)

(͡° ͜ʖ ͡°)

AVERAGE JOE

The strangest thing
Just happened to me
I was looking at a girl
And then…
Her boyfriend!

Boyfriends everywhere.

And all with their stupid faces
And all with their empty heads.

Boyfriends with my girls.

Ugly boyfriends with my girls
Boring boyfriends with my girls.

Everywhere

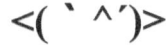

BRUCE LEE

Walking through the city street
Looking at the sky
Feeling free
Spending the whole weekend
In a forest
At home
On the beach.

In a mind sown with green
The present comes as a present
To you
Today
To me
For real
For free.

@}-;-'---

BUKOWSKI

when I meet a woman
and I want to fuck her
well
she's always married
she's always buried
she's always married.

I feel I need a bitch.

sometimes
when she's just simply retard
well
then I realize I need some whore
so hard

<(` ^´)>

PINK MOON

The night
With its whores
It's like my heart
With its jokes:

Strolling down a highway
Full of cars
And lights.

No smiles.

~ °._.° ~

DREAM #69

Green
I love you green
Over the flowers
Underneath me
A road
Stroll.

Yellow
I feel it yellow
Sunny
No shadows behind me
No memories haunting me
I drift… and then I fly…

Blue
Love in her eyes
Naked sky
Alive
Alive
God high fives

(/● ７ ●)/

FATHER

Going down to the sea
Where we used to swim
With the dolphined dolphins
With our heads full of dreams.

It's been a long decade of nights
No wife awaits home with a smile
And I complain for the lack of future
But nobody knows why
She would smile to me.

She floats through the breeze
Between the rocks of the beach
In this final sunset movie scene
With a pearl and a bird
On her candied pink chest
As a nest.

I don't care 'cause she doesn't care!
Do you ever care?
Do you anyone care?

Where are you for me?
Where is she for me?
Where is everybody?
(~_~✗)

IN THE AEROPLANE OVER THE SEA

My fiancée dumped me
A fat American hates my French guts
Would a priest lock his church for me?

Flight fare
Flight ticket.

Fly
Fly on the wall
And so will I
Come on.

C'mon
C'mon
C'mon
(☞° ７°)☞⇀☜(° ７° ☜)

GREED IS GOD

Everybody wants to win the lottery
I want to win the lottery, everybody
You want to win all the lotteries everyday
The rest is sex.

ヽ(´ー`)┌

SHARK

Don't you drink the water
Til it turns into lead!

Don't you drink the water
Until it becomes red!

< (((" >

I LIED

I know
Nothing
About love
About sex
About myself.

I only cry...

*I lied
Oh I lied!
I lied...*

((+_+))

LOFT STORY

Coming back from work
You better not look at me
Believe me
You may find out who I really am
Believe me
You don't wanna see.

You don't wanna see
The desert in me
Better eat a dessert
While watching my huge TV.

I love you the way you are
Hot as an edible sun
But you love me like another story.

Love story
Loft story
((+_+))

LOVE SEX DUREX

Love…

… Or just some sex
With a whore
Or a normal girl
If you can find her…

… I never did
And when I did
I did not do…
… Anything...
((+_+))

LOVELY LOVE SONG

I'm in love again
Hello sexy friend
♪♪♪

Easy rhyme
Not a crime
♪♪♪

When you're in love
Poetry is your own loft
♪♪♪

Now there's more to see:
Dolphins dolphing in the sea
♪♪♪

Happy rhyme
In my mind
♪♪♪

Love calls
Waterfalls
♪♪♪

Donkey
Monkey

I am in love
♪♪♪

Punky
Junkie
You are not
♪♪♪

Love:
A land
In the palm
Of a hand
♪♪♪

Love:
Jam
In a gram
Of beach sand
♪ ┌(·o·)┘ ♪ └(·o·) ┐

MARK DAVID CHAPMAN'S SONG

What is wrong, John
With me just loving you?
I am just a fan
Who wants your autograph...
♪♪♪

Your Japanese wife is so adorable
I have one for myself too
Isn't it a miracle?

What is wrong, John
With me just loving you?
Just loving you (x2)
♪♪♪

It's so great that you thought of me
To write your songs
I feel every single time I listen to 'em
Like one of your sons.

What is wrong, John
With me just loving you?
Just loving you (x2)
♪♪♪

Your band was so fantastic

That I need a narcotic…

What is wrong, John
With me just loving you?
Imagine the sad things that a cold gun
Oh, could do…
♪♪♪

What is wrong, John, what is wrong?
What is wrong, John?
What is wrong with you?

All you are saying is
Give peace a chance
So be my girl
In a last lap dance
♪♪♪

What is wrong, John?
What is wrong?
What is wrong, John?
What is wrong with me?
What is wrong, John?
What is wrong with me just loving you?

Just loving you (x4)
//0-0\\

MATTRESS ACTRESS

Japanese goddess
Jacuzzi
Bikini.

Champagne running through her veins
Dom Pérignon in her hand
Waiting for me and the sun.

First drink of the day.

Drink of the year.

Smile of the decade.

Love of my life
(/● ⊃ ●)/

MY BED

My bed
Condoms
Menstrual blood stains.

My bed
Breakup
Outbreak.

My bed
Post-Duchamp readymade
Autobiographical
Confessional
Every part of me's bleeding.

My bed
Not yours
Nor his
Nor hers
Nor theirs.

MY bed
Critics
Plebeians.

MY bed
Never done before

Never before seen.

Modern
Original
Shocking.

Contemporary art.

P.S. Thank you
Bowie
Charles
YOU understand
(❀^‿^)

SMELLS LIKE KURDT COB

Swimming down the street
Smoking ice coffee on TV
Kissing a gay fish.

Yeah, yeah, yeah, yeah
♪ ┌(·o·)┘ ♪ └(·o·)┐

On top of this beautiful starry night
I washed an old couple of parasites.

Yeah, yeah, yeah, yeah
♪ ┌(·o·)┘ ♪ └(·o·)┐

In an endless dream
Deers are hunting me
While your ghost hugs my penis.

Yeah, yeah, yeah, yeah
((d[-_-]b))

NO SUICIDE

Don't kill yourself
Whoever you are
Please
I'll hug you
Disguised as a giant panda
We'll eat something
Drink something else
Fall asleep
For a day
Not eternity

And cry tears of joy
And laugh about it all
The morning after
Remembering what happened
(^_-)

OSHO

I wish more
I want more
I feel so bad
I feel so hollow
I feel so weak.

Now I have more
Now I fear more
Maybe an alarm
Keeps away the harm.

I don't want more
I don't wish more
I feel so warm.
I feel so calm.

Now I'm so much more myself
Now I break the cell of the shell.

In life you are a player
In love you are a prayer.

The sun was waiting for
My flower-like life to open up
So from this moment on I'll sing along
@}-;-'---

PEACE & LOVE

Roses are a threat
Violets are a fluke
I kiss U2
(❀^‿^)

PINK

There'll be blood on the cleaver tonight
It has been said and I won't say it again
There'll be blood on the cleaver tonight!
I've had to break the ice twice
Because of the frozen sea
You have inside
Sonny boy
Try to understand.

You are not only going to stay up
All night
Thinking about all those meals
You've had blindfolded
Throughout your life
The way I saw a clot
For the very first time in mine
That is
Seeing red
I'm so very sorry to say
But burning the midnight oil too
Creating new savoury recipes
To substitute
Some ingredient
Which is only normal
After the initial shock.

The important thing
I've been trying
To tell
You
All along
Is…
That…
Bacon
Isn't
Made of
Wheat
But
Meat!!
That was it.

It is as delicious as the colourful
Cheerios
you must be munching while
Reading this poem
I know
I have butterflies in my stomach too
Every time my tongue senses it
And my teeth grasp it
And my teeth tear it
But truth exists
Despite our hearts
So white
And truth is always salty

Fruit of my loins
As you just have discovered.
(´_>`)

RAP MESSIAH

Big brother
Let's stare at each other
♪ ┌(·o·)┘ ♪ └(·o·)┐

Contemporary poet
Why not rhyming
Why stop it
Easy rhyme
Not a crime
Life is calling
Lief is waterfallin'.
♪ ┌(·o·)┘ ♪ └(·o·)┐

Sandy
Handymany
Hand my granny
Sunny
Funny
Sunday
Money
♪ ┌(·o·)┘ ♪ └(·o·)┐

RAP THIS POEM

dunno drink da water
til it comes red
dont u drink my blood ya dawg!!
wow da heel wrong wit cha??
ヽ(´ー`×)ノ

ROAD MOVIE

Highway
Highway.

A homeless thumbing
A cactus smiling.

Driving
Driving.

Jack's hands on the steering wheel
It's all about the feel
I'm with my gal in the back of the car
Doing hot stuff.

Sun
Sun.

Straight, Jack
Good luck.

Landscape
Landscape.

The breeze in our tears
The freeze in our years
My heart on her sigh

Her breasts on my side.

Highway
Driving
Sun
Landscape.

My way
Living
Sunday
Escape
☞(∩ ▽ ∩)☞

NO ROOTS

No roots
One ticket
Nowhere
Home
((+_+))

SEX SELLS

Hello
I'm nice
Sex sells
Alright
(/●ヮ●)/

160 IQ

Tired of being smarter than you
Just don't know what to do
Beat my head against the wall?
Drink cough syrup??
(°ᴧ°)

SMELLS LIKE SEXY PARTY

Suck my dick
Patti Smith.

I have no lyrics
I am free.

Lick my dick
Party Myth.

Yes I have no groupies
But I am free.

Rimbaud loves ME
Party Smith.

Suck my dick
You Myth!

Oh eat my dick
Now bitch!!

Because the night belongs to me!!!
♪ ┌(·o·)┘ ♪ └(·o·) ┐

THE POET

The poet killed himself violently
Out of boredom and laziness.

The poet was messed up
A mix of everything.

With a white heart and a golden soul
White trash.

A poet despite his poetry
A philosopher who only trusted his gut.

A serious comedian
Either too nice or too mean
Empathetic to others… living in his head
More genuine when posing
Out of character in his own biopic
Painter who loved writing haiku
Writer who preferred contemporary art.

With too many pennames to have a name
His worst lines are now the best
Too crazy to be a fool
Tense and anxious yet lacking ambition.

Chasing ideals without an idea

Coming back without having left
Lost everywhere.

A strange person
Capable of everything —good at nothing
Courageous —fearing dullness.

A cursed poet
So misunderstood… by himself
Never was anyone nor anything
Wanting to do nothing —had multiple jobs
So corrupted… that it made him naïve
Similar to all… but himself
So himself —unbearable for himself
Feeling disgust —he treasured that.

My epitaph:
He died the way he lived:
Expecting to finally start living
@>-->--
@}-;-'---
@>-->--

ROCK 'N' ROLL

I can tell by the way I feel
You're no good baby
It's surreal
I can tell by the way I feel
You're not good with me babe
Crystal clear
(^_^) o 自自 o (^_^)

VOLLMANN

I don't need you more
And no alcohol
I don't need your smiles
I now need more
And your hugs
They are not enough.

I only want my dick
Inside someone else
And poetry about myself
And her lips between my legs
And my body over her
And her body over mine.

I only love touch control
I adore touch contact.

What about her eyes?
No compliments
With money she's mine
No questions asked
(͡° ͜ʖ ͡°)

ROLLINS BAND

I think I could die!
If I tell you
How much I love you
And then I ask you for a date
And you say *No, it's too late* ♪♪♪

I would whisper in your ear
So many adventurous
Beautiful
Plans
But I can't pretend I don't know
That at the end you'll say:
No, go to the gym or bed:
I will date the family man! ♪♪♪

I think I could die!
I think you should die!! ♪♪♪

I'm so sorry!
I can't meet you out of the 'Net!!
I live there!!! ♪♪♪

DIE!!!

\(o`Ⅲ'✘)/

WEIRD AL YANKOVIC

'Cause you are a star full of skies
I want to swim in your eyes
♪ ┌(·o·)┘ ♪ └(·o·)┐

I don't care if you are a star made of cereal
I don't care if the skies are for flying
'Cause you are a star full of fries
I want to fish in your eyes
♪ ┌(·o·)┘ ♪ └(·o·)┐

www.ingramcontent.com/pod-product-compliance
Lightning Source LLC
Chambersburg PA
CBHW031546210526
45464CB00003B/1181